MARTIAL ARTS

MARTIAL ARTS: PHYSICAL DEVELOPMENT

BRYANT LLOYD

The Rourke Press, Inc.
Vero Beach, Florida 32964

Consultant for this series: Michael T. Neil, master instructor of Korean Martial Arts; head instructor of Mike Neil's Traditional Martial Arts Centers, Batavia, IL.

EDITORIAL SERVICES:
Penworthy Learning Systems

Library of Congress Cataloging-in-Publication Data

Lloyd, Bryant. 1942-
   Martial arts—physical development / Bryant Lloyd.
      p. cm. — (Martial arts)
   Includes index.
   Summary: Focuses on the specific ways that martial arts training can help improve physical development.
   ISBN 1-57103-231-2
   1. Martial arts—Juvenile literature. [1. Martial arts—Training.] I. Title
II. Series: Lloyd, Bryant. 1942- Martial arts.
GV1101.L626 1998
796.8—dc21
                                        98–22411
                                           CIP
                                           AC

TABLE OF CONTENTS

BALANCE

Martial arts (MAHR shul AHRTS) training can help you develop, or improve, your physical condition. Martial arts training also helps you use your body skillfully in **self-defense** (SELF duh FENTS).

Balance, for example, is part of martial arts training. With proper balance a martial artist can move quickly. If you're attacking, defending, or even falling, you can have control over your body.

You learn good balance skills by learning how to stand and shift your weight.

Early karate artists understood the importance of using their legs in martial arts combat for more reach and strength.

Learning how to stand and shift your weight improves your balance control.

POSTURE & STANCE

   Balance is likely to follow if you learn posture and stances. Martial arts teach proper posture. You learn how to position the upper **torso** (TAWR so) of your body. You also learn how to tuck in your hips, keeping your torso and hips in balance.

Martial artists stand in back stance (left) and front stance (right).

Learning to stand properly leads to good posture.

A stance is the way you position yourself when you stand. Each stance—front, back, and side—has its proper use and advantages.

COORDINATION

Coordination (ko awr duh NAY shun) is using various body parts together to complete a task. If you're hitting a baseball, your wrists, eyes, and feet need to work together closely.

Coordination allows martial artists to make the proper movements for self-defense. Training helps put "all the pieces together"—breathing, vision, muscle strength, balance, and the movement of hands and feet. Being able to focus your mind properly on a task is part of coordination, too.

Coordination requires focusing on a task as well as a partnership of muscles, eyes, lungs, balance, and movement.

SPEED & DISTANCE CONTROL

As a martial artist, you want to control the distance between yourself and your opponent. If you have short arms, for example, you need to be close enough to throw punches. Your hand and foot speed is a large part of your ability to control distance.

Martial arts training helps you learn to move cat-quick from a relaxed position into a strike. You also learn not to signal, or "telegraph," a move before you strike.

Martial artists do speed drills so that they can react quickly and properly to any attack.

Even a martial artist who holds a black belt can learn more about the art. Within the black belt class are additional learning levels, called "degrees."

Martial artists practice speed and distance control.

SELF-DEFENSE

Martial artists learn to be fighters—but only when they need to be. They don't look for fights. They try to avoid fights. But martial arts like tang soo do were developed long ago so that people could defend themselves if attacked.

Martial artist (left) practices self-defense with a wrist-control technique on her opponent.

Martial arts training gives students of the arts confidence in their ability to defend themselves.

Knowing they can handle themselves against a physical attack gives young martial artists confidence. That confidence in their ability gives them the mental strength to walk away from verbal attacks.

TRAINING

Martial arts training helps your body strengthen itself in many ways. Part of that training is called **cardiovascular** (kahr dee o VAS quh lur). Cardiovascular workouts help your heart and lungs.

Your heart is a muscle. It pumps blood, which carries oxygen. Like any muscle, the heart can be strengthened by exercise. A strong heart works better than a weak one.

Your lungs can build a greater area for drawing in air. That leads to more breathing control and endurance.

The word "judo" means "the gentle way." Judo teaches how one can use the least amount of effort to overcome great force. Hitting, kicking, and striking are forbidden in judo.

Cardiovascular workout strengthens the heart and builds endurance.

ENDURANCE

The purpose of cardiovascular workouts is to build endurance. Physical activity requires endurance, and it also builds it.

Endurance is your ability to do something for a longer time than you did it before. You may be able to do just two push-ups today. As you build endurance, the number of push-ups increases.

You will always have a "failure point." That's the point at which you can't do any more. But by improving endurance, you can change your failure point.

Hard work and sweat lead to greater endurance.

MUSCLES & STRENGTH

Strength is needed for balance and endurance. Like other physical activities, martial arts training helps the body build and condition muscles. Conditioned, or trained, muscles gain strength and work the way they should for what you want them to do.

Exercises help martial arts students warm and condition muscles.

Strength-building exercises are part of martial arts training.

Many martial arts systems today use weights in training to improve strength. For centuries, though, martial arts training depended upon people lifting and pushing only their own w

WEIGHT CONTROL

A martial artist wants a body weight that's healthy for that person. Martial arts training is not designed to help people lose weight. But most overweight people do lose weight when they begin training. More important, martial arts training helps a martial artist keep fit muscles and a steady weight. A steady weight tends to be the weight that is healthy for the person.

Many people not involved in physical training find that their weight see-saws up and down. Regular training in martial arts, as in other physical programs, stops the see-sawing.

Gichi
is som koshi, from Okinawa,
modern alled the father of
5 feet, 1 Funakoshi was only
centimeters) tall.

P.

tivity in martial arts training helps control weight.

GLOSSARY

cardiovascular (kahr dee o VAS quh lur) — having to do with the heart and blood vessels

coordination (ko awr duh NAY shun) — the ability to use various parts of the body at the same time for a single purpose

martial arts (MAHR shul AHRTS) — the many systems of fighting, or combat, using mainly the hands and feet

self-defense (SELF duh FENTS) — the skill of defending oneself against attack

torso (TAWR so) — the trunk of a human body; the body except for the head, arms, and legs

Physical training helps a student become a martial artist.

INDEX

FURTHER READING

Find out more about martial arts with these helpful books and information sites:
Armentrout, David. *Martial Arts.* Rourke, 1997.
Blot, Pierre. *Karate for Beginners.* Sterling, 1996.
Potts, Steve. *Learning Martial Arts.* Capstone, 1996.
American Judo and Jujitsu Federation online at—http://www.ajjf.org/ajjf.html
Martial Arts Menu page online at—
   http://www.mindspring.com/~mamcgee/martial.arts./htm/
Martial Arts Resource page online at—
   http://www.middlebury.edu/~jswan/martial.arts/ma.html
Shotokan Karate International (SKIF) USA Headquarters online at—
   http://www.csun.edu/~hbcsc302/